CAREERS IN SCIENCE

What Do GEOLOGISTS Do?

BENJAMIN PROUDFIT

PowerKiDS press
NEW YORK

Published in 2022 by The Rosen Publishing Group, Inc.
29 East 21st Street, New York, NY 10010

First Edition

Portions of this work were originally authored by Ryan Nagelhout and published as *Be a Geologist!* All new material in this edition was authored by Benjamin Proudfit.

Editor: Greg Roza
Book Design: Michael Flynn

Photo Credits: Cover Jorge Guerrero/Shutterstock.com; (background texture) Anna Timoshenko/Shutterstock.com; p. 4 prill/iStock/Getty Images; p. 5 Chris Howes/Canopy/Getty Images; p. 6 National Galleries of Scotland/Hulton Fine Art Collection/Getty Images; p. 7 Mark Godden/Shutterstock.com; p. 8 ttsz/iStock/Getty Images; p. 9 Lloyd Cluff/Corbis Documentary/Getty Images; p. 11 Don White/E+/Getty Images; p. 13 Smith Collection/Gado/Archive Photos/Getty Images; p. 15 Sean Gallup/Getty Images; p. 17 Jacek Sopotnicki/iStock/Getty Images; p. 18 zaferkizilkaya/Shutterstock.com; p. 19 technotr/E+/Getty Images; pp. 21, 24 Monty Rakusen/Cultura/Getty Images; p. 23 Bloomberg/Getty Images; p. 25 Danita Delimont/Gallo Images/Getty Images; pp. 26, 27 courtesy of NASA; p. 29 Harald Sund/Photographer's Choice/Getty Images.

Library of Congress Cataloging-in-Publication Data

Names: Proudfit, Benjamin, author.
Title: What do geologists do? / Benjamin Proudfit.
Description: New York : PowerKids Press, [2022] | Series: Careers in
    science | Includes index.
Identifiers: LCCN 2020040289 | ISBN 9781725329553 (library binding) | ISBN
    9781725329539 (paperback) | ISBN 9781725329546 (6 pack)
Subjects: LCSH: Geologists--Juvenile literature. | Geology--Vocational
    guidance--Juvenile literature.
Classification: LCC QE34 .P77 2022 | DDC 551.023--dc23
LC record available at https://lccn.loc.gov/2020040289

Manufactured in the United States of America

Some of the images in this book illustrate individuals who are models. The depictions do not imply actual situations or events.

CPSIA Compliance Information: Batch #CSPK22. For further information contact Rosen Publishing, New York, New York at 1-800-237-9932.

Find us on

CONTENTS

EARTH SCIENTISTS

Whether geologists are out in the field observing Earth's features or **analyzing** rocks and **minerals** in the lab, they're important scientists! Geology has to do with studying Earth, what it's made of, its features, and its history, including how it has changed over time. The word "geology" comes from the Latin word *geologia*, which means "the study of Earth."

Earth is a big subject to study! That's why geologists choose a specfic area of geology. They may spend a lot of time doing **research**, or they may work for a private company finding the best place to build something. No matter what a geologist chooses to do, they have an exciting career in science!

From **fossils** to caves, there are so many areas of geology for scientists to study!

GEOLOGY'S HISTORY

The ancient Greeks made observations about Earth as far back as the fourth century. The ancient Romans mined certain rocks, like marble, to build their huge empire. By the 1700s, people were uncovering fossils. They used them to start understanding the history of Earth. In the 1800s, scientists started studying minerals more as mining became a big part of many countries' economies.

EARTH'S LAYERS

Hutton observed that rocks formed in layers, with different colors and types of rock lying on top of each other. He noted how slowly these layers take shape over time. He also described how they form and break down continuously as a "great geological cycle." Hutton thought changes on Earth were caused by heat coming from under the ground. Today, this cycle is called the rock cycle.

James Hutton

The first modern geologist was James Hutton, born in 1726. He studied chemistry and medicine but became a farmer. Hutton became interested in how weather changed his farmland each year. Many people during Hutton's time thought Earth was only about 6,000 years old. Hutton suggested the planet was much older than that. He believed that rocks were continuously breaking down and forming new rocks.

Hutton used rocks at Siccar Point in Scotland to support his ideas. Siccar Point features two different types of rock layers slanting in different directions. Its makeup suggested to Hutton that the layers formed at different time periods in Earth's history.

tectonic plates

North American plate

Juan de Fuca plate

North American plate

Eurasian plate

Caribbean plate

Arabian plate

Indian plate

Philippine plate

Cocos plate

African plate

Pacific plate

South American plate

Easter plate

Nazca plate

Australian plate

Juan Fernandez plate

Scotia plate

Antarctic plate

Hutton's most famous **theory** states that Earth is being shaped by the same processes today as it always has been. These changes happen at the same slow rate as well. Before Hutton's theory, scientists believed quick, powerful events such as floods formed and changed Earth. Over time, Hutton's ideas were accepted and built on by other scientists.

In the 1900s, Alfred Wegener proposed the next big geological idea: continental drift. This theory states that the continents, which are part of Earth's outer crust, have moved around Earth over time. They used to be one big continent called Pangaea! His work led to the theory of plate tectonics, or the idea that Earth's outer layer is made up of many moving pieces.

EARTH'S PLATES

Earth's outer layer is made up of broken pieces, or plates, that slowly move. There are dozens of plates. The major continents rest on the biggest plates. These "tectonic" plates move many different ways. They can grind past each other and cause earthquakes. Some push together to create mountains. They can move continents closer together or farther apart. By studying movements in the past, geologists can **predict** where the continents will move in the future.

The places where tectonic plates meet are called faults. The San Andreas fault, shown here, is where the North American plate and the Pacific plate meet.

BECOMING A GEOLOGIST

Geology has come a long way in the past 100 years! That means there's a lot to learn.

In order to do well in the field of geology, focusing on math, sciences, geography, and writing classes is important starting in high school. Gaining knowledge in computers is very helpful too.

Geologists need to earn a four-year college degree. They may choose to major in geology but also study math, history, and many other kinds of science. Many geologists stay in school to earn a master's degree, or an even higher degree called a doctoral degree. This can mean up to 10 years in school! Geologists with the most education often become the leaders of important research teams or work at colleges.

While in school, future geologists may have a chance to study some of Earth's coolest features, such as the hot springs at Yellowstone National Park in Wyoming.

TYPES OF GEOLOGIST

During their many years of study, geologists choose an area of geology to specialize in. That means they'll become an expert! Many specialties have to do with physical geology, or the study of the features of Earth and the cycles and processes that act on Earth's features.

Volcanologists are geologists who study volcanoes and the processes that take place under Earth to make them erupt. They try to predict when volcanoes may erupt, which can save lives. Some volcanologists study underwater volcanoes! Since volcanic rock can be full of valuable minerals, some mining businesses are interested in hiring these geologists.

Some geologists focus on earthquakes. They're called seismologists. Paleoseismology is the study of **prehistoric** earthquakes. Paleoseismologists study the timing, location, and size of these earthquakes.

WORKING TOGETHER

All sciences are collaborative. That means scientists often work together in order to find out more! Geologists are no different. Volcanologists and seismologists may collaborate on studying an area known for many volcanoes and earthquakes. It's likely they'll see what other scientists have studied in the area, too, from meteorologists—or scientists who study weather—to physicists!

Volcanologists' job can be dangerous if they're studying a volcano that's actively erupting!

Mineralogists are geologists that study minerals. They often study those that are mined, like iron ore, copper, or aluminum. They may also study gems! Mineralogists find out the properties of rocks and minerals, including how they withstand pressure and heat. Petrologists are similar to mineralogists. They study rocks! Petrologists may further specialize in one of the three main kinds of rock: sedimentary, igneous, and metamorphic.

EARTH'S ROCKS

TYPE OF ROCK	HOW IT FORMS	EXAMPLES
SEDIMENTARY	PRESSURE BUILDS OVER TIME, PRESSING TOGETHER **SEDIMENT** AND OTHER MATTER	SANDSTONE, LIMESTONE
IGNEOUS	HOT LAVA COOLS AND HARDENS	BASALT, OBSIDIAN
METAMORPHIC	HEAT AND/OR PRESSURE CHANGES EXISTING ROCKS	MARBLE, GNEISS

Another form of geology doesn't focus on rocks at all. Glacial geologists, or glaciologists, study ice, including snow, sea ice, glaciers, and ice sheets. They examine how snow and ice affect Earth today as well as how they affected it in the past. Glaciologists often work in places like Antarctica, Greenland, and the Arctic.

Glaciologists often study the changes in glaciers over time. This information can tell scientists about how Earth's climate may be changing.

Another main area of geology is historical geology, which is the study of the history of Earth. Historical geologists want to find out what Earth was like millions of years ago. They work to understand how Earth formed. They also want to know the main events that changed life on Earth and the features of Earth itself. This can help today's scientists better understand how global climate changes occurring today may affect Earth and its features in the future.

The field of geology is as deep as Earth's core! Marine geology, environmental geology, and engineering geology are just a few other specialties one might study.

Historical geologists can learn a lot from studying Earth's features, such as the Grand Canyon, shown here.

PALEONTOLOGY

Paleontologists study the life on Earth that existed millions of years ago in order to find out more about Earth at those times. They use fossils, including where they were found on Earth and in rock **strata**, to uncover the mysteries of Earth's past. Paleontology has a lot to do with geology, but it may also be considered part of biology, or the study of living things.

FIELDWORK

No matter what specialty a geologist chooses, their work will likely have two main parts: fieldwork, and lab and office work. Fieldwork is the study and observation geologists do at a certain site, or place. Geologists commonly work as part of a team when out in the field.

Geologists map the site they're studying. They note the different rocks they find and the physical features of the area. They look to see how the features seem to interact. Geologists may take samples of the rocks or soil they find. Everything they see and find is recorded. The notes geologists take in the field are used later.

A geologist's fieldwork could take them deep into a cave or even underwater!

TAKING ON THE FIELD

Successful fieldwork depends on many things. Sometimes the weather isn't good or the **terrain** is tough to work on. Geologists need to be master problem-solvers in the field as well as knowledgeable about what they are studying. They need to be ready for rain, wildlife, and other challenges that may come up when they are in the field.

TO THE LAB!

Many geologists spend a good deal of time in a lab analyzing what they've found. They may use tools to examine any samples they've brought back from the field to find out what they're made of. Geologists also use special ways of dating these samples in order to find out how old they are.

Geologists then record and **interpret** their findings. They may use computer models to better look at what they've found. Often, geologists write up reports of what they're studying. This may include publishing their findings and theories in a journal. Publishing can be a big part of a scientist's work. It shares new ideas with other scientists who may be able to build on their work.

Using **technology** is a big part of geological study today.

WORKING IN INDUSTRY

Most geologists find jobs working in industry. Geologists who work for mining companies locate valuable minerals, called ores, in the ground and figure out the best way to remove them. Ores may be valuable themselves or valuable for what they contain, such as the elements copper, silver, or gold. Geologists also help make maps for constructing tunnels and plan methods for workers to remove ores.

Energy companies need geologists to locate fuel sources such as natural gas, coal, and oil. Geologists can find new sources of oil and gas by collecting and analyzing samples of rock and soil. If they're like samples found near known deposits of oil and gas, there may be an oil supply nearby.

Natural gas, coal, and oil are called fossil fuels. They form over millions of years as a result of great pressure on plant and animal remains buried deep within Earth. Geologists know the best way to find them!

JOB OUTLOOK

There are plenty of geology jobs for those who graduate from college with degrees in geology. In fact, there are likely more jobs available than there are geologists to fill them! However, those looking for jobs in their specialized field of geology might need to be willing to move to where a job is, rather than finding one nearby.

emerald mine

When a town or company wants to build a new school or lay a new road, they'll often work with a geologist. These engineering geologists often work for private companies that specialize in helping choose and prepare sites for construction. They learn about the land that's being considered and give advice about the best places to build and what materials would work best in the soil and rock of the area.

Though many geologists work for private companies, they may do their own research too. They may be able to use findings from their job, or they may do other research on the side. Another way to do geological research is working at a college. Some geologists work full-time as teachers at a college too.

Incredible geological sites like Cathedral Gorge in Australia draw both geologists who want to study them and visitors who just think they're amazing!

GEOLOGISTS IN SPACE?

Another major employer of geologists is the U.S. government. One of the most exciting places a geologist can work is the National Aeronautics and Space Administration (NASA). They apply their knowledge of Earth to learn about other planets, moons, and space objects. After all, these are made of the same matter as Earth! Sometimes these geologists are called astrogeologists.

Harrison Schmitt earned a doctoral degree in geology and worked as an astrogeologist before he walked on the moon!

Harrison Schmitt was the twelfth and last person to walk on the moon. He's also the only geologist to visit the moon! Schmitt worked for NASA and went to the moon with the Apollo 17 space mission, landing on December 11, 1972.

ROVING MARS

Scientists are finding out a lot about Mars with the help of a machine called a rover. It travels on the planet's surface, takes photos, and collects rock samples. It can actually analyze the rocks too. Geologists now believe that Mars has plate tectonics, just like Earth. Imagine what astrogeologists will find out next!

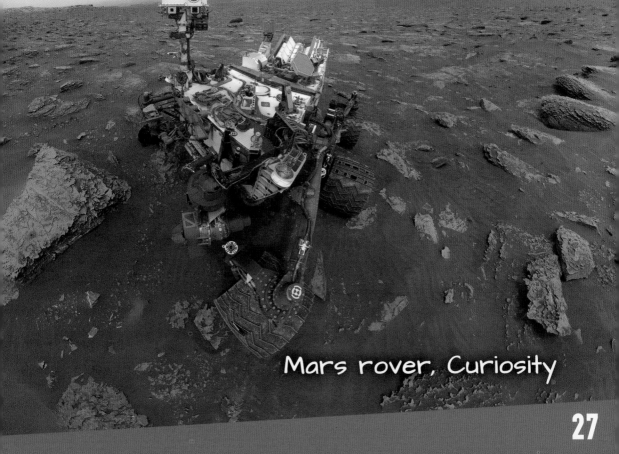

Mars rover, Curiosity

IMPORTANT SCIENTISTS

You don't have to wait until college to start studying geology. It's a science you can work at right in your own backyard. Start by looking at the soil in your garden. Is it rocky? Or is it more like clay? You can also visit any interesting landforms near your house, whether you're near mountains, a rocky beach, or even cliffs! Take notes on what you see and have an adult help you look up more information when you get home.

Geologists have an important job. They learn about Earth's past and Earth today and then explain to us what may happen to our planet in the future. These curious scientists can have a long and interesting career!

If you want to know more about becoming a geologist, you may be able to find one to talk to! Have an adult help you look up nearby colleges and private companies where geologists might work.

GLOSSARY

analyze: To study something closely and carefully.

fossil: The marks or remains of plants and animals that formed over thousands or millions of years.

interpret: To find the meaning of something.

mineral: Matter in the ground that forms rocks.

predict: To guess what will happen based on facts or knowledge.

prehistoric: Having to do with the time before written history.

research: Studying to find something new.

sediment: Matter, such as stones and sand, that is carried onto land or into the water by wind, water, or land movement.

stratum: One of many layers of something, such as rock. The plural is strata.

technology: Using science, engineering, and other industries to invent useful tools or to solve problems. Also, a machine, piece of equipment, or method created by technology.

terrain: The type of land in an area.

theory: An explanation based on facts that is generally accepted by scientists.

FOR MORE INFORMATION

BOOKS

Ball, Amy, and Florence Bullough. *The Rocking Book of Rocks: An Illustrated Guide to Everything Rocks, Gems, and Minerals.* Minneapolis, MN: Wide Eyed Editions, 2019.

Wolny, Philip. *Geologists at Work.* New York, NY: Britannica Educational Publishing in association with Rosen Educational Services, 2018.

WEBSITES

Geology 101
kids.nationalgeographic.com/explore/science/geology-101/
Learn much more about geology and see amazing photographs of Earth's natural features.

Geology
online.kidsdiscover.com/unit/geology
This website covers many important geological topics, from fossils to meteors.

Publisher's note to educators and parents: Our editors have carefully reviewed these websites to ensure that they are suitable for students. Many websites change frequently, however, and we cannot guarantee that a site's future contents will continue to meet our high standards of quality and educational value. Be advised that students should be closely supervised whenever they access the Internet.

INDEX